Destiny

True Friends Are Rubies

Ogooluwa Jimi-Peters

JDD Books

Destiny

True Friends are Rubies

Published by JDD Books

+447309255086

Book Cover: artistrykal@gmail.com

Contents

INTRODUCTION

TRUE FRIENDS

'True' means real or exact, especially when this is different from something else. 'Friend' means a person you know well and like who is not usually a member of your family. A true friend is someone you can tell your secret or talk to when in danger.

A true friend can be:

- A brother or sister

- A confidant

- A helper
- Your classmate

Steps in choosing a true friend.

- Look for a person that is friendly.
- Watch the person and his/her dealings.
- Make sure he/she is not a pretender.
- Make sure he/she is kind or nice.

We are going to look at what 'true friends' is in the lives of these two friends; Charles and Kelvin.

CHAPTER ONE

THE SEARCH

Once upon a time, there was a boy named Kelvin. He lived with his parents in a village, he helped his parents in doing the house chores. He has three siblings. Kelvin was attending a private school which was very far from his house, his parents chose this school for him because the fee is moderate for their low income and he had to trek from his house to the school everyday.

One day, while Kelvin was going to school, he saw a boy in his father's car going to school also and the boy asked Kelvin to come and join them. Kelvin had never noticed this boy before now, though they were in the same class. All the same, the car stopped for him and he entered. The boy introduced him to his father as his classmate in school. The boy later asked for Kelvin's name and he said, "My name is Kelvin. And yours?" "My name is Charles, nice meeting you, Kelvin", said Charles. "Can we be friends?" Charles asked. "Yes of course". Replied Kelvin. They began to laugh and when they reached the school, they got down from the car and thanked Mr. Alex, Charles' father for bringing them to school.

When it was assembly time, all the children rushed out when they heard the bell. Charles and Kelvin held their hands as they walked to the assembly. After the assembly, the two friends sat quietly in their classroom while other pupils were making noise. Suddenly, two boys and a girl walked up to them and said facing Charles, “who is this boy Charles? Is it because of him that you are no more playing and shouting with us?” Then he said yes, “he has asked me not to be playing around in the class, so what is your business?” Then the two boys said he cannot be his friend and they began to push Kelvin from the seat, but they could not because Charles was holding him. The two boys then faced Charles and said, “let's get rid of this boy for you so you can play with us.” When he did not answer them, one of them faced Kelvin and said, “you, we’re coming back for you!” And they walked away.

Mr. Jack, the English teacher, came in and saw Charles and Kelvin sitting down while other students were making noise. He asked the whole class except Charles and Kelvin not to go out for break that day, as punishment for making noise. After the teacher had taught them, he gave them class work. Charles and Kelvin did their work without copying one another. When they had completed their work, they submitted and went for break, while others remained in the class.

When the break was over, the two friends came back to the class and their mates became jealous of them. When the bell rang for closing, all the pupils left the classroom one after the other while Charles and Kelvin were waiting for Mr. Alex to come and pick them. As they were expecting Charles' father, Kelvin advised that they start reading their books before the arrival of Charles' father. As they were reading, Mr. Alex arrived, and they ran to meet him. The father faced his son and said, "you can follow me and, pointing to Kelvin, you go to your house." His son did not allow his friend to go; rather, he insisted that Kelvin must follow them, if not, he too will walk home with his friend. The father reluctantly accepted. When the boy got to where he would drop, the father shouted, "get out of my car!" Kelvin got down from the car and said, "thank you so much sir", but Mr. Alex drove away without saying a word. He didn't say anything to his son either, till they got home even when his son was thanking him for driving him home as usual.

On getting to the house, Charles greeted his mum and went straight to his room without talking to anybody, not even his siblings. The mother later sent the house girl to him so he could come and eat his food, but she came back to report that he said he was not ready to eat.

Sensing that something was wrong with his son, Mrs. Alex went upstairs to meet him and asked him why he would not eat his favorite meal. That was when Charles opened up to his mum by telling her everything that happened back at school.

He said he saw his best friend on his way to school in the morning and asked his father to wait and pick him up with his car, which he did. However, in the afternoon, his father asked his friend to trek to his house as he wouldn't allow him to enter his car. He added that he had to insist on following his friend on legs if he wasn't allowed to enter the car and that was when his dad reluctantly allowed him in. He went further by saying his dad shouted at his friend to get out of the car when the boy got to his bus stop and that he refused to answer the boy when he was thanking him and saying goodbye to him.

The mother said, “is that why you don’t want to eat, my son? Go downstairs and eat your food as I will sort things out with your dad.” Charles was so happy and he said, "thank you mum,” as he hugged his mother and rushed downstairs to eat his food.

After eating, Charles’ mum announced to him that the two of them would go to his friend’s house. He was so happy and quickly rushed upstairs to dress up.

“Mum, do you know Kelvin’s house?”, asked Charles. “When we get to his bus stop, we shall ask”, answered his mother.

His mother took a piece of cake and some money. She announced to Charles’ father that she and Charles were going out, she took her car key and drove off. When they got to the junction where Charles’ father dropped Kelvin, they asked people living around that place about Kelvin, with his description and school uniform people were able to recognize who they were looking for easily, so they were directed to his place, without wasting time.

As they were going, Charles saw him afar off with a tray on his head, he was hawking oranges. Then Charles said "Mum, look here, see my friend coming, that's Kelvin selling oranges"! His mum then parked the car and they both went down to meet Kelvin. "Good evening my son," said Mrs. Alex. Kelvin shyly responded, "Good evening ma". "How are you?" Asked Mrs. Alex. "I'm very well, thank you ma". Kelvin responded. Charles then cut in, smiling, "I promised you that I will come and visit you in your house, I know you didn't believe me". "Thank you so much, you're indeed a good friend, I thought your dad wouldn't allow you to come and visit somebody like..." Mrs. Alex didn't allow

Kelvin to complete his statement when she interrupted him. “Oh Kelvin, are your parents at home?” “Yes, my mum is at home and my dad is yet to come back from work”. Answered Kelvin. “Okay, come and enter the car so we can go and visit them”. The two friends ran to the two back doors and as Mrs. Alex was helping Kelvin with the tray of oranges, asked him for the price of the remaining oranges and Kelvin told her. The woman then asked her to pack everything in a bag and she handed the money to him as she entered the car.

The two boys sat side by side beaming with joy of seeing one another again. It was Charles that first broke the silence. He said, “Kelvin, I’m very sorry with the way my dad treated you this afternoon”. Then Kelvin replied, “I felt bad about it, but I had to console myself that we would only be seeing one another in the school and there's no point following you home since your dad doesn't like that idea. I'm already used to trekking, it's not a big deal for me you know." Mrs. Alex then cut in, to defend her husband. "You know what, Kelvin, my husband doesn't hate you, he's just trying to be careful since your parents don't know us and that's why we're here, I bet with you after this visit, everything will be fine, Is that okay, my son?" Then Kelvin brightened up and said, "okay ma."

CHAPTER TWO

THE VISIT

When they got to their house, they greeted the Martins as his friend is Kelvin Martins. They were offered seats in their humble living room. Mrs. Alex told Kelvin's mother their mission, said that she came to know the house of her son's friend, as well as his parents. She also explained how happy his son has been since Kelvin has become his friend. She saw Kelvin's siblings too. as Kelvin is the second born of the family with three sisters and a brother, who is the last born. She handed the cake she brought for them to Kelvin's sisters and all of them including Charles went to play outside the house.

The two women were left alone in the living room and they were talking. Before long, Kelvin's elder sister had returned with four peeled oranges in a neat plate and put it on the only small stool in the living room and Mrs. Alex thanked her. Mrs. Alex then faced Mrs. Martins and said, "your children are well brought up" and went on that with her few hours with Kelvin, she can see that he is a very good boy and well brought up child too.

As they were talking, Kelvin's father, who works at the local post office as a clerk, came back from work and greeted the two women. They greeted him back and as he was about to go to the room, his wife quickly introduced Mrs. Alex to him as the mother of Kelvin's friend in school. He then turned back to greet her again before going inside with Kelvin carrying his office bag behind him. Mrs. Alex then told Mrs. Martins that she would be leaving and promised to come back. She then gave the money in her hand to Mrs. Martins. They both exchanged pleasantries and when they got outside, Mrs. Martins called out, "Charles! Your mum is ready to go". The two boys embraced themselves and all the children bade Charles and her mum farewell.

On their way to the car, Charles was so excited and said, mum I like Kelvin's house, they don't have money, but they seem to be happy. They have football and a frontage where they can play it. I think I love that, the children are so pleasant and accommodating.

As they entered the car, Mrs. Alex's phone rang and her husband was seriously raking at the other end of the phone, “you will explain to me where you went today. Where have you been since morning?” He didn’t allow the woman to respond before hanging the phone on her. She drove back home with mixed feelings and the boy too, understanding what was going on, kept mute throughout the journey.

On getting to the house, Charles’ father was already pacing around the big living room and as they entered, he faced his wife and asked in annoyance, “where have you been, woman? I ask again, “where did you go from 4:30pm and you are coming back by 8.30pm?” His wife replied, “I went to the house of Kelvin’s friend”. Now getting angrier, “How many times have I warned you not to allow my son to mix with God forsaken poor people like that? Tell me, how many times? Now look at me, the next time I hear you go to that house, you will be in trouble" and "you, now pointing to Charles, that boy is not your friend, he can never be your friend! Never!! He then stormed out of the living room without waiting for any response.

Mrs. Alex, knowing her husband very well, being already used to this type of outburst from him, just asked his son to go upstairs for his homework and come back for his dinner. Afterwards, she went to the kitchen to see what the house help and her two daughters were doing. "Good evening, madam", said the housemaid. "Good evening, what are you doing?" She asked, "The food is ready. I'm just cleaning the kitchen." Replied the housemaid. "Where are the girls? I told you to always engage them so they can know how to do these things. Go and call them for me." Mrs. Alex requested.

When Charles' sisters came, they chorused, "mummy you're welcome." "Welcome, so what are you doing upstairs that you didn't assist Derby with the supper? Don't let that repeat itself, you need to learn all these things so you can know how to do them. Besides, she must not be the only one doing everything in the house, is that okay?" "Okay mum", they both answered.

Mrs. Alex set the table for dinner, assisted with her two daughters and she went upstairs to call her husband, without referring to what had happened earlier. They all ate their food, chatting as they were eating, but their parents ate in silence.

Mrs. Alex was the first to wake up the following morning, to have her morning prayers after which she went to wake Derby up to give her some instructions. She asked her to put food in an extra lunch box for his son's friend.

As Mr. Alex was driving his son to school the following morning, his son asked him why he hate his friend and the man answered by saying, "see my son, I'm doing all these to protect you, Kelvin is from a poor family, I don't want you to move with poor people. Birds of a feather flock together, you both have nothing in common." "But dad, is it a crime to be poor? If they have the opportunity we have, they too can be rich. Besides, there are a lot of things we can also gain from them. Kelvin is my friend and I don't want to be separated from him." "You have to obey my instructions, I'm your father and I know more than you do, is that okay?" His father replied. "Dad, you haven't told me this boy's offence", queried Charles. His dad ignored him and as he was parking in front of the school, said “boy you’re running late for school, get down and hurry to your class, bye.” "Bye dad,” said Charles as he carried his bag and dragged his feet to the class.

CHAPTER THREE

THE TURN AROUND

Kelvin was the first to see his friend, he ran to meet him and said, "thank you for coming to my house yesterday, thank your mummy for the money also, my mum used it to pay the balance of my school fees this morning." Charles replied, "oh, about that! It is good to help. You know, what baffles me is, my dad doesn't want us to be friends, he wants me to move around with his friends' children, but I won't separate myself from you," I know it too, he doesn't like me because I'm from a poor home, I promise you, I won't break this friendship too," said Kelvin. Then, Charles opened his bag and gave Kelvin a pack of food and a bottle of water. With a smile on his face, Kelvin said thank you to his friend. After eating, the two of them went out to play. When they closed, Charles gave his friend some money for transport since his father won't allow him to follow them home. Kelvin went home, he didn't enter the cab but saved the money his friend gave him, Charles stayed behind to wait for his dad. When his father came, he was happy to see his son alone and the boy entered while they headed home. On getting home, Charles told his father thank you as usual. He went inside, greeted his mum, went upstairs, took his bath and came downstairs to eat. As he was eating his food, his father came to sit beside him and began to ask him questions, "how was school today?" The boy answered, "school was fine dad." "And who is your new friend?" His father asked again. Errm eeem Kelvin, the boy stammered a little before he could answer. Then the father got up in annoyance and shouted, "are you okay?" "Kelvin is still my friend, dad." Charles said this time raising his voice.

Then, Charles' mum came out from the kitchen and in a low voice, said, "honey, Charles is a responsible child." The father then faced his mum and said, "you're the one spoiling this boy" and stormed out of the living room. Charles began to cry and said, "I don't know why my dad doesn't like Kelvin. What did he do to him?"

His mum assured him that she would speak to his dad about it. Charles then told his mum that Kelvin has taught him how to read his books in the school instead of making trouble and disturbing the whole school along with his old friends.

"No wonder your teachers have stopped ringing my phone to report you," noted his mother. "Mum you know what? I'm planning to buy a gift for him for his birthday," Announced Charles.

"That's a good one but do you already know his birthday?" His mum asked. "No, I'm going to ask," answered Charles. "What if it has passed?" Questioned his mum. "That's true, I would ask tomorrow and if it has passed, I would look for an opportunity to give him some presents." That's fine, get up and go get your books, do your homework before you come back for your favourite games and TV shows. "Okay mum, I love you", said Charles and ran upstairs, before his mum could respond "Love you too my son."

When Destiny got home, he showed his parents the money his friend gave him, but his father was very angry with him and asked him to say the truth about the moneyhe would get mad at him. He then added that Charles' mum also sent food to him in school and the mother testified that his child was telling the truth. The father then collected the money and said, "I've asked God to send help to us today as I don't have any money to give your mother to get something for us to eat this night, I didn't know this is how God will do it". He then blessed God for the provision and gave the money to his wife to get something for dinner.

Kelvin's mother called Mrs. Alex to thank him, but it didn't go through. She then asked her son to thank the boy and extend her greetings to his mum too. He also warned his son not to collect money from the boy or anyone again.

The woman later called Mrs. Alex, told her everything her son told her, about the food and the money and she showed her appreciation for the show of love towards her son. She prayed for her that God would continue to bless her and her family.

She also asked if she could visit Mrs Alex and she said in the affirmative that she can come anytime, that her house is open and she would be happy to have her in her house.

When Mrs. Alex got to the room, she met her husband pacing up and down and she asked, “dear, what’s going on?” The husband then said, “Who was that friend you just asked to come to your house any day?” She replied, "oh, that was the mother of our son's best friend, nothing is wrong with that family, God can even use us to change their status.”

“Dear, everything is wrong with them, I've told you that I can't make people that are below my standard my friends, that's not possible! Mr. Alex shouted at his wife and he went to the bed. His wife just knelt down and prayed to God. She said, “Father, thank you for everything you've done for us, please God help us to be of help to those in need around us, open our eyes to know that you blessed us so that we can be blessings to others, in Jesus' name, I pray. Amen. After her prayers, she too went to lay on the bed beside her husband to sleep.

It was the husband that woke up his wife in the middle of the night and said, “honey I want to apologise for being harsh on you about the family of our son's friend, you said something that touched me yesterday, you said God blessed us so we can bless others. Since then, I've been thinking about how we can assist those people so they can get out of poverty, when did you say they're coming to visit us?" The wife answered, "oh thank you honey, I just asked her to come anytime she wishes to, but she would inform me before coming." "That's okay, let's prepare for their visit and let's welcome them to our home just like big people. Do you know I've been noticing changes in our son's life since he has started playing with this boy?" His wife then said, "yes, his teachers are no more reporting him to me unlike before." "So, it's a mutual benefit after all, there is a lot to gain from people around you, whether they have money or not." Mr. Alex said and continued, "I just learnt that it's not good to look down on anyone, as that person might be of help to you someday, please always pack extra food for the boy." The wife smiled and said, "thank you my dear, I will do that."

In the morning, Mr. Alex took his son to school as usual and asked to see Kelvin. When Kelvin came, he was afraid to see him, but Mr. Alex apologised for how he has been treating him and promised that he will not stop him from being his son's friend any longer. The boy said, “thank you sir.” As he was about to leave, Mr. Alex brought out some money to give him, but the boy did not collect it, he said his mum had warned him against collecting money from people. "Oh, boy this is coming from your friend's father," but the boy declined saying that his mum would be upset if he collects it.

As much as Mr. Alex was embarrassed with Kelvin’s action, he was also touched by the sense of responsibility and honesty his parents have imbibed in him. This made him love the boy more and he vowed to treat him just like his son, Charles.

CHAPTER FOUR

THE TRIAL

One day, the students were making noise in the class, but Kelvin and Charles were reading their books as usual. Their Chemistry teacher just entered the class and asked them to prepare for a test, that he would punish anyone that fails the test or whoever is found cheating. He spaced them so they won't copy one another.

When the test was going on, he went out and just as he was coming in, Kelvin stood up from where he sat. Unknown to him, his friend also stood up at the same time; they were both going to submit their answer sheets to the teacher who was about to enter the class. That was whensome students started shouting that the two friends were cheating, that they copied the answers directly from their textbooks. The whole class was in a total disarray that the teacher himself was confused. The teacher didn't listen to the two boys, instead he took them to the principal's office and reported that he caught the two friends cheating during the test. She added that no wonder the two of them, especially Charles, have been getting higher scores in their work recently.

The principal was so mad at them that he said he has been looking at the two of them as responsible children and now, they have disappointed him.

He picked up his phone and dialed the lines of the fathers of the two of them, asking them to report to the school immediately. It was Mr. Martins that came first, and the principal explained to him that the two friends have been suspended for two weeks due to exam malpractices and that he should wait to collect the letter as the secretary is already typing them. The principal continued by saying, "we don't want them to spoil the name of this school, they're going to serve as examples for others who are like them. You can bring them back after two weeks, after which they would be expelled from the school, if they refuse to change." Mr. Martins then said, "these children can't do this. Please Mr. Ali, can we investigate this matter?" The principal replied in the affirmative," there's nothing to investigate as the teacher caught them in the act." Mr. Martins became dumbfounded and decided to wait for the letter. As the principal announced that the letters were ready, Mr. Alex came in. Although Mr. Charles hadn't met him before, he recognised him immediately as Charles' father, as the two boys were still there and he knew the two of them had been friends for a while. So, he greeted Mr. Alex who just looked away from him. Going straight to the principal, he said, "Good afternoon Mr. Ali, what did you say my son did?" The principal handed one of the letters to him first, then the second to Mr. Martins who had been standing all this while and he said, "the two of them were caught cheating during a test session in their class." Without saying a word, Mr. Alex just looked from his son to Kelvin and stormed out of the principal's office with the letter in his hand.

Mr. Martins looked at Charles and told him to quickly go and get his bag so that his dad doesn't leave him behind." He then faced his son and said, "Kelvin, go and bring your bag, let's go home. Goodnight Mr. Ali." He left the office before Mr. Ali could say a word.

Mr. Alex was in the car reading the letter when the boy came to join him and he drove home without saying a word to Charles. Charles too didn't say a word as he could smell trouble already. Mr. Alex got home and started raining abuses and insults on his wife, "see what you've caused, I knew it that nothing good can come out of people like that, now you've succeeded in bringing our precious name into the mud, see yourself!" He threw the letter at his wife and went upstairs. The woman didn't say a word, she just picked up the letter from the floor and read it silently. When she was through, she went upstairs to meet her son who she was found crying profusely in her room.

"Mum, I didn't do it, but no one including dad wants to listen to me, my friend is innocent either..." He said amidst tears." "Son, wipe away your tears and explain to me what happened in detail," his mum interrupted him. He then explained how he and his friend were reading in the class while the other boys in the class were shouting and making noise and a teacher came to give them a test. He said according to the teacher, the noise was disturbing the whole school as he heard them from the staff room. He added that the teacher spaced all of them so that they would not copy from each other. He mentioned how the teacher went out to use the toilet and the big boys began to search their textbooks for answers and they were jumping from one table to the other to copy from their friends.

"It was at this point that I saw the teacher coming and I stood up from my seat to submit my script, as I've finished my work and was only waiting for him to come back. Unknown to me, Kelvin also stood up from his seat to go and submit at the same time, and that was when I heard, "they were cheating, Charles and Kelvin, copied from the textbooks." That was how the big boys in the class disorganized the test and started dragging the two of us to the front of the class." He explained and continued by saying, "the teacher did not allow them to talk, he just asked us to follow him to the principal's office and when he got there he explained to the principal that he caught us with textbooks in our hands. The principal became so annoyed that he asked us to kneel down and all explanations were to no avail." "Mummy, I… we're innocent," now sobbing profusely." By this time, Mrs. Alex too had become emotional, she held his son to her chest and assured him that everything would be taken care of, as she believes her son.

When Mr. Martins told his wife what happened and showed him the letter, Mrs. Martins stood up and started asking his son questions, "why did you do this to us, you were not like this before or what came over you?" Charles was already crying, and he explained everything that happened. His father was the first to talk and he told his son not to worry as he would get to the root of the matter.

CHAPTER FIVE

THE VINDICATION

The following morning, during the devotion, Mr. Martins asked the family members to pray about what happened to Kelvin, that God should give them clarity about the whole matter. As he was about to leave home for the office, he told his wife that he would go to Kelvin's school during the break time.

On getting to Kelvin's school, Mr. Martins went straight to the principal's office. After greeting him, the principal said, “oh, good morning Mr. Martins, hope your son is becoming sober now, you see we have to...” Mr. Martin's did not allow him to finish his statement when he said, “please can I see Kelvin’s Chemistry teacher who conducted the test for them yesterday?” “Sure, you can, please have your seat while I send somebody to call him.” Before long, the teacher was already in the principal’s office. “Good morning sir,”he greeted the principal. “Good morning Mr. Omoyele, this is Mr. Martins, Kelvin’s father, he’s here to see you,” responded the principal. “Oh, good morning Mr. Martins, how may I help you?” The teacher asked. Mr. Martins responded, “good morning ma’am, I want us to talk about what happened in your Chemistry class yesterday. Mr. Ali, can you please excuse us? Let me see him outside." "No worries, if that's what you want," said the principal.

"Please Mr. Omoyele, is it true that you caught these boys with their textbooks when the test was going on yesterday?" After hesitating for a while, he said, "em, em, actually, I met the two of them standing up when I entered their class because I briefly dashed out of the class to ease myself, as the test was going on, but their mates confirmed it when I entered their class by showing me the textbooks they were coping from. As a matter of fact, I've been watching the two of them for the sudden change in their performances recently, especially Charles, someone who was so poor before now, even till the beginning of this session, that he would either score zero or one out of ten, now he's getting nine or ten out of ten. Isn't that questionable? So, the reason for his recent change was just confirmed by this act." Mr. Martins was able to get some facts from Mr. Omoyele's story, that she just believed the students to confirm what was already going on in his mind. He then requested to see one of the responsible students who witnessed the whole scenario yesterday.

Mr Omoyele immediately asked a student who was passing by to call Janet for him. On arrival, Janet greeted both of them. Mr. Martins introduced himself as Kelvin's father, you can see the fear on the girl's face when she heard this. Mr. Martins then said, "you don't have to worry my daughter as there's nothing to be afraid of." With this assurance, Mr. Martins continued, "Janet can you please tell me exactly what happened during your Chemistry test yesterday, that led to the suspension of two of your classmates Kelvin and Charles. Please tell me the whole truth".

The girl then adjusted her dress and began by saying, "I was not one of them sir, but let me say the truth. Kelvin and Charles are friends and they were always reading their books even while others were playing in the class. Also, there are some boys in our class who are always bullying people and causing trouble, they've been saying they would set the two friends up one day. So yesterday, when our teacher went out of the class as the test was going on, these other boys started copying answers from their textbooks and copying from one another. However, the two friends stood up at the same time the teacher was coming in, I don't know what they were doing, but they stood up from their separate seats, almost at the same time, that was how these other boys put the textbooks in front of them and said that they were cheating and, and…" "Thank you Janet, it's okay, I've gotten what I needed to get." Now facing Mr. Omoyele, Mr Martins said, "you must not mention this girl's name to anyone as no one must know how I got this information, it is left for your school authority to do the needful to get the boys. Janet, thank you very much, you can go." Janet thanked Mr. Martins and left. By now Mr. Omoyele was already ashamed of himself and was begging him not to tell the principal, but Mr. Martins insisted that the teacher follow him to the principal's office.

Mr. Martins asked the teacher to narrate the story to the principal. The principal as well as the teacher felt bad about their hasty decisions. The principal blamed the teacher for misleading him and for leaving the class while a test was going on without asking someone to stand in for him.

He then went to the class and announced that the whole students would be punished if they didn't speak the truth. That was how the culprits were mentioned and the principal expelled them from the school.

Then he called Mr. Alex to come to the school at once, as his son had been vindicated. The principal apologised to Mr. Martins and asked him to let his son resume school immediately. The principal thanked him, and he left.

When Mr. Alex came, he was so furious, he said nothing would make him leave his son in such school again and he left in anger. The principal asked Mr. Omoyele to write apology letters to the parents and he was issued a query afterwards.

On getting home, Mr. Alex explained what happened to his wife, he apologised to his wife and son. He then requested that they pay the Martins a visit without telling them what he was going there to do.

When they got to the Martins' house, Charles had gone to hawk bananas, and as they were greeting his parents, he returned with a few pieces of banana on his head.

Mr. Alex apologised for all that happened and how he didn't greet Mr. Martins when they met at the principal's office a day before. He then announced that he doesn't want the children to attend the same school any longer that he would personally go and enroll the two of them in a new school which is better than their current one. He added that he would appreciate it if Kelvin can be allowed to come and live with them or at least be coming to their house for holidays. He added that his house has become theirs as they are now family friends. The Martins were so happy with this decision and they promised that Kelvin would be coming for holidays.

CHAPTER SIX

TRUE FRIENDS ARE RUBIES INDEED!

As promised, Mr. Alex came to their house with Charles and his wife in the car, before 7.00 am the following morning to pick Kelvin so that he could go and enroll them. Mrs. Martins followed them, while her husband was preparing to go to work.

On getting to the school, Mr. Alex paid the bills for the two of them, they were given their uniform, textbooks, and notebooks and were asked to go to their class immediately.

Mr. Alex promised to pick them up after school everyday. He dropped Mrs. Martins at home and he also gave her some money.

The new school coupled with the relationship between the two families encouraged these boys and by the end of the session their performance had greatly improved as the two of them were leading the class. Mr. Alex used his influence to get a good job for Mr. Martins and both families were doing well.

They sat for their final exams in high school and they did excellently well. They were both given admission to read medicine in one of the best universities in the country. The two friends were so inseparable that throughout their studies, nothing was allowed to come in between them. They also graduated with first class with a lot of awards.

A big hospital in the country also offered them immediate employment.

On the day of their graduation, Mr. Martins could not hide his feelings as he was just pouring blessings on his son for the fame he had brought unto the family through his friend. Mr. Alex was also appreciating Charles for his decision of a true friend that turned him to a serious and focused child.

The two friends were very happy, the two mothers also wore the same dresses, and they were grinning from ear to ear.

As they were about to cut the graduation cake, Charles whispered to Kelvin's ear, "thank you for being a true friend...," Kelvin didn't allow him to land when he said, "Charles, you're the true friend here, I owe it all to you."

OGOOLUWA JIMI-PETERS

www.ingramcontent.com/pod-product-compliance
Lightning Source LLC
LaVergne TN
LVHW041251150826
845673LV00008B/2537